for those who

silently endured adversities
stood bravely amongst all odds
smiled when their hearts wept
shone brightest amidst darkness!

Sabina Oberoi

REVIEWS

'String of Memories' is an anthology of reflections; a wondrous journey through the labyrinthine mind; at once a quittance in remorse, yet a quest into unfulfilled. Sabina Oberoi's poetry is deep and sensuously desultory embedded in the mysterious to be savored by the seasoned.

VINOD PANDE, Indian film director, producer, writer, actor

'String of Memories,' Sabina Oberoi's compilation of poems, are lived and deeply personal. They navigate her life and experiences in the language of poetry. The melancholy setting within the poems also carries an accompanying philosophical and spiritual strength of lived and living thoughts.

APARAJITA KRISHNA, writer, journalist, and creative-collaborator

Sabina Oberoi's poems in 'String of Memories,' explore a gamut of emotions like love, gratitude, and include unpleasant ones like loss, jealousy, and guilt. Pining for a lost love or celebrating a present one, with reflections on life interspersed in between, some tell a story, while others make you pause, perchance to think and reflect, on one's own life journey. There is a universality in the language, simple yet empathic, evoking similar emotions, on memories past or experiences lived. A thought-provoking read for a quiet Saturday evening.

MINAL NIRMAL KHONA, writer, editor

'String of Memories,' by Sabina Oberoi, are strokes of memories painted on her poetic canvas. Each poem draws from deeper hues of love or loss, passion or pain, hope or hate or friendship or deceit.
With each verse comes an invitation to delve deeper into the experience behind the memory…

COLLEEN D'SOUZA, HR professional & poet

PREFACE

'String of Memories,' a collection of poems reminiscing
about the past, gingering up a myriad of memories, some
shyly and others craftily concealed in the exclusive, inner
space. We may live in the present pushing back the
innumerable shades of grey and hues of colours from the
past, yet these remembrances from yester-years sustains us
as we wobble towards the twilight days of our lives…the
rustle of leaves, rain-drops, sudden gust of wind, whiff of a
familiar perfume, feelings of love, jealously, rejection,
these lie intricately stringed to memories, framing an
integral part of the persona, growth, and evolvement, filling
the being with nostalgia; sometimes brimming the eyes
with tears of happiness and joy, other times with sorrow
and pain, but keeping us alive…

Sabina Oberoi

Contents

JUST ONE MISTAKE

The time is gone forever

Never to be lived again

That something special you'd given

Before I made that mistake

Is lost far into the horizon

Never to be felt again

I lost what I had gained

For that one mistake.

Guilt will tear me apart

Never letting go

A constant ugly reminder

Clinging like a ghost

If I was granted one erasure

Just one last chance

I'd erase the mistake with all my might

And forever clean out the heart.

MORE AND MORE

2

There's nothing more to want
Once I've gazed at you
Then I want a wee bit more
And continue to want more and more...

SLEEP LOVE, SLEEP FOREVER

Tenderly, holding her warm body in my arms

Lying down smoothly under the moonlit palms

Hearing her soft breathing musically in my ears

Holding on to her tightly, I weep quiet tears

Sleeping daintily, looking so pure and divine

Touching face, wishing she had been all mine

Lovely woman of mine living on borrowed time

Poisoned by me and slowly dying in her prime

Saw my best friend and her drinking wine

Jealousy, madness, taunted and tainted mind

He kissing nape of neck, she stroking with palms

Now am seeing her dying with last glass of wine

MIND IS MASTER

We're trapped and enslaved
By the dictates of the mind
'Coz, we have made our mind the master

LIVE THEM EVERYDAY

Desperately pushing the thoughts away

Embedded in the deep recesses of the mind

Which crawl out to haunt the present

Creating a dangerous web inside

Sweating with fear and guilt

Feeling threatened!

But hold on...

Who can comprehend the mind?

Who can experience those feelings?

Who can heal the fragmented soul?

Who can touch the spaces hidden?

No need to deprive or push thoughts away

Live them, live them every single day

I GREW WEEDS

You planted seeds
of peace and love
I grew weeds
of selfishness and distrust
'tis now a treacherous journey
seeking entrance to Divinity

MEMORIES

Buried in the depths of the mind,

mysterious experiences

of dreams disintegrated

of feelings trapped,

concealed, numbed, and wrapped.

Sometimes shuddering

other times softly flowing

Like ocean in its womb hiding

Or mountain belly silently masking

Caged memories in the mind suppressing

DISCIPLINE THE MIND

A mind that is disciplined

has the ability

to control

and

discriminate

PROTECTOR

Ignorant, unknowing I am about you
your mysterious, protective ways
feel you standing firmly with me
when I silently weep within

Your presence is invisibly experienced
During hard times grip is tightened
When from the mud you lifted me
Tenderly cared, washed, and loved me.

Moments I was alone, helplessly incomplete
You straightened my back, got me to my feet
You shadowed me silently in your absence
Whispering sweet words to me.

SEE-SAW

Life is like a see-saw
Full of highs and lows
Lows build character
Highs inflate ego

NATURE'S WRATH

Eyes closed in deep meditation

Serenity beyond comprehension

Monk worshipped by villagers

Believing in his endeavors

One night the thunder came

Skies opened, cried, and wailed

Young girl was raped, murdered

Monk was found guilty and butchered

Silently he sat through the brutality

While life drained out of him quietly

That night the thunder came again

Washed people, fields, and cattle away

Guilty was found, left his footprint

Young girl's neighbor was culprit

Only a few were left to tell the story

Of God's messenger destroyed blindly.

BELIEVE

Think and then believe
Believe and then speak

TRUSTING LOVE

Every week Gloria a letter receiving

From boyfriend who was absconding

Police were frantically searching

Twenty-one-year-old who was running

Ten years later and still he was absenting

Pressures on her for good boys marrying

She was adamant and kept on refusing

Patience finally paid off her years of waiting

He arrived in town one bright sunny morning

Scooping Gloria in arms, passionately kissing

'I didn't steal anything then I am promising

Now stealing this girl whom I am marrying.'

BLIND FAITH

Blind Faith is freedom
Coz it is unlimited
by its nature of being blind
Spirituality is having the resilience
through meditation
changing blind faith to conviction

ROOTED DEEP

Dreamily weaved our lives

Lazily on the beach

Built a beautiful home, had two kids

Chalked their careers, got them married

Happily, waited to be grandparents

Then

Came the big wave, washing away dreams

No home, kids, career, or marriage

Neither were we grandparents

Sandy shore swept him clean

And I remained a story on the beach

MIGHTY ONE

His might can't be defied
Believing wrong is right
Wrong may be right for us
His right is the ultimate might

RELATIONSHIPS

17

Relationships are not perfect

Adjusting to imperfections

Polishes relationships to perfection

FRIENDSHIP

We met in school when we were six

Immediately struck a unique friendship

Played little pranks and silly games

Cried together when we felt homesick.

Entered adolescence showing-off breasts

Compared whose was bigger and best

Laughed over schoolgirl crushes

Sneaking love letters to other's boyfriends.

Hanging Nun's undies in dormitories

Getting beaten and sent to infirmary

Oh, those happy, carefree, fun-filled days

With youth and energy, bright and gay

WORDS

19

Harsh words reflect

lack of control

of the mind

NOT A POET

I'm no poet, I do admit
And boast not of this skill
Lacking in Paltu's intensity
Sultan Bahu's sensitivity
Meera Bai's devotion
Dear Kabir's adoration
Bulleh Shahs' wild madness
Ravi Dass's sincere sadness
None of them intimidate me
From writing my own poetry
Whether songs, words, or prose
Or in crazy dis-jointed verse
Write I by my gut level instinct
And say it just the way I feel it
I don't mean to be rude or vain
But do add Sahib to each name
Omitted for poetic limitations
I'm lacking in so many ways

REMOVE SHACKLES

21

Remove the shackles
of others' perceptions
Be free to live
by your own convictions

TODAY ONLY

Love today
Tomorrow is unseen
Be compassionate today
Yesterday is a gone dream
Feed a hungry mouth today
His smile will last an eternity

WE WEAVED DREAMS

In every lane and park, on buses and cars

School and college cafés or restaurants,

Fun times when we talked and laughed

Rain drenched wet embraces

Hands in each other's pockets

Stolen kisses behind doors

Endless telephone talks

Sharing drinks from a single straw

Sun tanning on the shore

Biking to a weekend resort

Cycling together to the store

People smiling on the streets

Two lovers sharing ice-cream

Sharing joys and sorrows

Aging into blissful retirement

Together we weaved dreams

LONGING FOR YOU

Eons of heart-ache

Pain and tears

Sleepless nights

And deep fears,

Soul is torn apart

With pain,

Uneasy, crying out

your name

CLINGING TO MEMORIES

Each person in this lazy, old town

Ruminates on our tender love song

Reliving the frightening, dreadful day

Of two young lives that sadly frayed

Fragmented, torn, forever separated

Shattering, butchering loving hearts

They brought home the tattered body

Ice-cold, still, lifeless, and bloody

I crumbled seeing the man I loved

Helplessly lying in a pool of blood

One leg crushed, one shoe on

Black hair dabbed with dried blood

Numb with pain I turned away

My broken heart buried with him

Life cruelly snatched my love from me

Left me clinging only to memories

EVOLVE

26

Evolvement emerges

from

the depths of despair

SINFUL

So graciously you took my hand
Tenderly cared and nurtured
But knowingly I sinned
Tainting forever
the purity of the love
You showered

Gorge the eyes, rip the heart,
Tear the flesh, pulp each bone
And let them burn!

Let the flames rise high
Burn the heart that held desire
Leave no traces
Burn, scald, churn, turn to ashes,
Keep the smoke away
Lest others are sprayed
With my sinful ways.

ATTITUDE

When we change
our attitude,
Our true
learning starts

OSTRACISED

I feel ostracized,
cruelly, coldly,
ruthlessly thrown
in the back of beyond
neglected, unloved
insecure, homeless,
deprived and down under

YEARNING

Wearily walking

Sun scorching

Sole burning

Eyes scalding

Heart yearning

Soul craving

To unite with Thee

PASSIONS OF THE MIND

Fiery five passions of the mind
Lust, anger, attachment, ego, and greed
Cancerous roots require elimination
With perseverance and determination

Mad, passionate, burning, lecherous lust
Imbalances, weakens, deprives true love
Difficult to escape this wild, tricky net
Trapping and shackling even the best

Senseless, dangerous anger wipes
Precious relations and friendly ties
Wiping mind of rationality or sanity
Destroying and sweeping away dignity

Attachment releases fear and instability
Restlessness of both mind and body
Stiflingly and suffocating the soul
Knotted in superfluous, chaotic mold

Friend to no one, the eccentric ego
Building importance of its very own
Portraying and thriving only on self
Selfishly maniacal, disastrous effects

Greed, the ever dampener of the soul
Perpetually dissatisfied at every goal
Shackling, crippling, confining, owning
Possessing, restricting, always craving

MEDITATE

Meditation is a process that
strips our mental barriers,
turning them into greater
dimensions within

SWEET MEMORIES

We dreamed dreams

That were never to be

No roses bloomed my way

Nor children in fields played

Joys and sorrows left unshared

Aged into retirement by myself

Memories sadly linger on and on

Of the one I loved, now long gone

Sweet memories are alive with me

Take into my coffin, before setting free

SURRENDER

The Supreme Power
Takes the reins in his hands,
When we surrender
and submit to him,
That's the exact moment he
Connects with the soul

NO CONTROL

I've handed myself to you
Do with me as you please
I have no control
Thoughts are only of you
Mind is lost
Cannot frame any other thought
But of you!
Completely consumed with you
Walking, sleeping, crying
Thoughts flow only of you
Mold me anyway you wish
Take over my entire being

INSANE LOVE

Every drop of blood
squeezed from the being
fills me with madness,
as I insanely seek
your love for me

BROKEN PROMISE

You made me a promise once
But never kept up to it
I think of it ever so often
And each time the throbbing starts again

Now even if you did, as you said you'd do
It wouldn't quite be the same
For the moment has passed
And will never come again

KILL THE MIND

Break all bondages, set soul free

Kill the mind; when empty and clean

Float with sound to great heights

Experience bliss deep inside

Conquer mind! Prepare to die

Die whilst the mind is alive

HURTING ME

Your words reverberate in my ears
Unable to absorb them, how they pierce
Like a leech sucking out every feeling
Exhausted, dejected, broken and weeping

Can not fathom why you want to hurt me
How could you reject my love and despise me
Painful memory of your words will ring forever
'Words are meant to hurt you' reverberate in ear

FORGIVENESS

Forgiveness is by givers
Cleansing the soul
Unforgiveness by fools
Adding to woes

WAVES

Contemplating the calmness of the waves

gently caressing, kissing the sandy shore

so tranquil, serene, and submissive!

Same calm waves brutally rise high to devour

vicious, forceful, and aggressive

swallowing all that dares its wrath!

Like human beings; murderers,' or priests

placid, destructive, pacifiers or aggressors

wait and attack like unsuspecting waves!

DECEIT

Lies, deceit, treachery,
Venomous - volcanic
Dissipates integrity

SENSE NONSENSE

43

The mind struggles with a matter
Matter distorts to chatter
Tries to rake sense
But the sense is nonsense
Mind, matter, chatter, sense, nonsense
Indulgence of mind's idol-ness

LONELY AND LOST

My loneliness is not
connected with people
Am lonely and lost
amongst them all
Craving for you is
permeating the insides
tearing it apart
only you can release
the pain and loneliness
by capturing my heart

EGO

45

Step down the ego

To step up self-esteem

BEAUTY

Beauty is not meaningless things
What to wear
How to look
Color of hair or
Dressing fingers and toes
Beauty is quite simple
'Tis about purity of the soul

POWERFUL TONGUE

The tongue is a powerful
weapon,
It can destroy a
relationship with harsh
words or
defuse it with
comforting words

COMPENSATION

Every tree has a branch
Every branch a leaf
Every bird has a nest
Where it nests a family
Every fuel lights a fire
Fie warms the hearth
Every river has a bed
And sleeps in it's depth
Every boat has a shore
The shore has a beach
What compensation dear life
Have you given me?

DIVINITY

Experience His divinity
By accepting, not resisting,
By submitting, not defying,
By giving, not receiving
'tis not a barter
'Tis faith tested with time

WILL YOU...

When I need a friend
And some understanding
Perhaps a little compassion
And maybe some hugging
When eyes flow with tears
And heart cries and weeps
When I need to vent feelings
Will you be there for me?

FAITH AND DOUBT

Faith and doubt
shackling shadows
enticingly entwining
twirling n trapping
appearing
disappearing
when one is
the other is not

FEEL DETACHED

Some change has taken over
From all I feel detached
When others talk with me
I'm sleep-walking thru the act

Not aware if dead or alive
Function like a robot
Limbless, lifeless, uninterested
In the happenings around

Am alive only when you appear
Life comes flowing back
Rainbow comes proudly in bright colors
Brightening the dullness everywhere

NURTURE LOVE

Love escapes

when

Nurturing fails

NO PURPOSE

I have failed in everything I've done
From an innocent child to a grown-up
Life's circle has culminated into nothing
A waste of life which has been fruitless
Why was I born if there was no purpose
With no direction, proper aim, or anchor
Just blowing away like the wind in anger
Even the role of a woman I could not play
That of a devoted disciple, daughter, sister,
Or of a friend, bride, wife, or mother
Then for what purpose was I brought here
Living like death is almost there at the door
So temptingly near yet teasingly far
Dragging the feet to get nearer and nearer
While it's moving further and further

LOVE

Love is not a singular feeling
Standing alone
Love is a combination of feelings
Blending to make whole

DON'T BETRAY ME

I've slowly amputated every part of me
To prove my love for you
I've shown what my love can do for you
In every way I could
'Tis time now for you to show me
That you're there too for me
Show me you feel, watch, and listen
Don't betray me

SPASMS OF PAIN

57

Each pore cries out in spasms

Aches of unbearable separation

Weeping, tearing eyes with tears

Crying for ever-lasting union

NO BETTER TIME

I need an anchor firmly by my side
And there's no better time than this
Done best to convince you of my love
Now a response is needed
Changed myself coz of my love for you
Time you gave some back too!

SADNESS

I'm aware of the intense pain
Rippling through every pore
There is always a sadness within
Which I do not understand at all

COME HOME

When night falls
shadows desert me
am totally alone
only with me
I need you then
Come home to me

HEART BLEEDS

61

Why my heart bleeds everyday
Or cries and weeps incessantly
Why there is a sad loneliness
Despite people around me

RESTLESSNESS

Why do I find myself alone
With a mad craving within
Why can't I decipher
This crazy restlessness

LUMPS OF SILENCE

When you are gone, in your absence
pangs of separation fill the veins
experiencing a painful, sad emptiness
beyond all noises, deep within,
I listen to lumps of silence.

GRIEF

Wandering in a dark barren world
Each day empty, bland, so utterly cold
Heart rips apart every thread of pain
The tremors of breath do not go away
Wounds of the eyes do not heal
Grief in the heart, scabs do not peel

ANOTHER WOUND

65

Each new day rakes
another wound
another burning
another scathing flame
Meaning of life drops asunder
Life from heart effaced forever

LISTEN

I have my share of problems
No one relates with them
Need to vent my feelings
Empty the loneliness
Release pent-up emotions
With a cry or two
Express thoughts that flow
But who will understand...

EERIE SILENCE

In your long absences
My whole being wilts
No joyous moment
no desire fulfilled
all is vacant and empty
only an eerie silence remains

CRAZED

I hear your voice
I'm crazed
Bursting with joy
Beyond myself
Joy and happiness again
Fulfillment, ecstasy
Life comes alive
I'm no more alone

CHAMELEON

Weary of these appearances
Tired of this pretentious life
Of all the chameleon colors
People change from time to time

CLOAK ME

Saw you for a fleeting moment
our eyes met
was captured forever!
Your presence ensnared me
cloak me like your shadow
don't release me!

ACHING FOR YOU

Bare trees

fallen leaves

twigs dried

shriveled

feel dead

tears dried

eyes scald

heart burns

insides call

plead, beg,

yearn, ache

for you again

HOW AND WHY

Birth spontaneously sows the seed

For death, the final eventuality

Where to be born, or when or how to die

'Tis a mystery, cannot fathom how and why

SHATTERED

You let me down
Hurt lingers painfully
In whom I gave so willingly
Took me ever so lightly

It's been etched in my mind forever
Inked with blood of pain
Every fiber and vein weep deeply
Tired eyes have dried with pain

TWO FEEBLE WOMEN

Two feeble women in last leg of innings

Laugh at white hair from nose popping

Crib of the other's obnoxious snoring

Muttering, grumbling about farting

Complaining which bone aches most

Argue whose dentures are in the bowl

While one's spectacle spring gets broken

Others hearing-aid battery is deadened

Fondly remember those young, firm breasts

Which hang loose now, way past their chests

Tight pants and jeans are a gone dream now

Wear only loose clothing with no undies on

In old age they enjoy each other's company

Sadly, aware one will out-live the other finally

WEB OF FANTASY

His ghost has enslaved me
Slyly and quietly, he visits,
Desperately I cling to him,
He evades and escapes
Setting himself free
A vicious web of fantasy

SAD IRONY

Bringing me down from my high horse is a sad irony
The appearance is deceptive, only a few can see
Result of deep-rooted insecurities no one can read
I need you to understand that part of me

DON'T DUMP ME

It's a long lonely road,

I need you at every stage

I'll falter, but be there

to hold and guide always

In the depths of my mind

and the core of my being

I want you desperately,

so don't dump me

IMPRINTED IN THE MIND

Promises held closely in my being
For fear they might run away
But they did escape me
Your promises did not see the day

My love, how could you speak words
And then not see them through
Because all the words you spoke
Were imprinted in the mind for good

PRECIOUS MEMORIES

79

Let me not waste precious time tonight

Savor each moment, slowing down time

Caressing with tender, sweet voice in ears

Softly whispering sweet love words to her

Gently touching her bare skin with soft lips

Collecting precious memories for the warship

SPEWING ANGER

80

Spewing anger with thunderous voice

Depletes words of wisdom and poise

LIFE'S PATTERN

Good, bad happens

Whatever happens

Whenever it happens

However it happens

Accept life 's pattern

With fortitude n determination

CANNOT REVERSE

82

Anger is reactive, cannot be reversed

Sometimes they hurt others

Sometimes they hurt us

Other times they hurt both

COMPLICATED MIND

83

The intriguing characteristic

of the human mind is to

make simple things complicated and

complicated things more complex

PATH OF IGNORANCE

We often choose the path of ignorance

because we tend to cling

to the phantoms of the physical,

instead of striving to achieve

something higher that is

not subject to change and decay.

FACT OF LIFE

Both despair and euphoria

about death are an evasion,

it is neither depressing nor exciting;

it is simply a fact of life!

FEAR

Illusions stem from fear!

Fear of the unknown,

Death, living, acceptance,

rejection, illness, poverty

and fear itself!

FORM OF ESCAPISM

We are gripped with fear

comforting ourselves with illusions

creating myths

as a form of escapism from realism.

POISONING THE BEING

Wounds from anger festers within

Poisoning the being

Heal the anger with awareness

Changing it by watching the mind

ALONE AND EMPTY

89

All attachments are illusions!

With one sweep life comes to a grinding halt

nothing belongs to us, nothing is forever!

When the final moment comes

when death knocks on the door

no relationship of any kind or

materialism of any sort accompanies

We leave alone and empty handed!

EVERYONE PERISHES

90

There is no belonging

in this transitory world

everything, everyone perishes.

DROP THEM

91

Learn art of letting go

of unpleasant situations,

pain and hurt

Cling not to situations and feelings

Drop them. Let them go!

Release unnecessary baggage.

Detach from attachment.

WILT AWAY

92

Materialism can be enjoyed

without obsessiveness or possessiveness

Power, name, fame will wilt away to the grave

MIRE OF ATTACHMENT

93

Crawl out of the mire

of attachment with detachment

Detachment has both sadness and joy in it;

sadness coz of the futility of wasted time

joy coz of greater vision that begins to unfold

when we let go.

POSITIVE ATTITUDE

94

A positive attitude manifests

in constructive, creative thinking,

energizing deep sorrows

into patterns of goodness,

weaving beauty out of ashes

and peace out of adversity.

HEAVEN WITHIN

95

An attitude of being

humane and compassionate

are qualities we need to imbibe

to create a heaven within us.

PRECONCIEVED NOTIONS

96

Attitude changes when we open

the mind and heart by disentangling it

from preconceived notions.

ACCEPT, NOT RESIST

97

Attitude is to accept, not resist;

learn, not question;

give, not receive;

let go, not expect.

DAWN

98

It's the dawn of awakening

when a change slowly creeps within

and the strange feeling

is incomprehensible!

REASON, LOGIC

99

Awareness turns the mind

to reason and logic

before it takes action.

PEACEFUL SPACE

When the mind stops fluttering,

it enters a peaceful space,

a state of awareness.

BALANCED MIND

Rocking, swaying mind blows with the wind,

casually drifting away

A balanced mind can stabilise and anchor it

PERSPECTIVE

The approach to issues is extremely emotional,

highly devotional or frantically passionate,

nothing substantial achieved with unnatural
feelings,

it requires a balanced perspective.

CHANGE

Change represents life,

existence,

development,

enrichment and elevation.

CHANGE IS EVOLVING

Change is happening every second.

changing every moment

cells in body decaying

expressions on faces changing

fading eyesight, deteriorating hearing,

falling teeth; change is evolving

NATURE OF CREATION

The nature of creation is to change,

seconds tick to minutes,

minutes to hours and hours to days.

The sun sets and the moon rises,

days move into nights,

the weather changes from summer,

spring, autumn, and winter,

there is perpetual movement and

change in every living being

and every part of creation.

LIFE IS MOVEMENT

Life is a movement like the waves,

continually moving day or night,

rain or shine,

the waves move on incessantly,

changing the intensity with high and low tide,

they never stand still,

there is continuous movement, continuous change.

JUST DO IT

When you make a commitment,

go ahead and do it!

Take the plunge!

Be bold and decisive.

Let nothing stop you. Just do it!

INNOVATIONS

We have the remarkable ability

to conceive convenient conceptions

and twist them into innovative interpretations.

INTRIGUING

The intriguing characteristic of the human mind

Is to make simple things complicated

and complicated things even more complex.

THE FINAL REST

The mystery of death intrigues each one of us,

we may guess, reason, study books,

stretch our imagination, but remain ignorant.

While it fascinates some, it scares others;

while some are obsessed with it, others fear it.

And some even deny it.

But it grips us all, it's the ultimate eventuality,

the only certainty, the end of all motion,

the final rest, death!

MOUNTAINOUS EGO

111

Break the mountainous ego

crush it to rubble

grind the rubble to sand

for the ego to be refined to humility

PERFECTION-LESS

Greed doesn't allow perfection to end,

it supersedes perfection.

Greed makes perfection perfect-less

MONEY

113

Money decides who our friends will be,

money decides who our family will be

worse, money decides who we will be.

CLOUDS OF ILLUSION

Our lives, relationships, and attachments

are like the clouds of illusion

that eventually evaporate and vanish too.

POLLUTED LOVE

115

When love demands conditions

It becomes polluted and impure.

EFFORTLESS FEELING

Love is a continuous,

incessant, effortless feeling;

cannot be quantified,

compartmentalized,

or rationed.

MOST COMPLEX

The complex mind is a

difficult machinery to tame;

requires enormous perseverance and dedication

to reach the point where it can stand

against adversity or calamity

without shaking from its roots

DISASTROUS AND DEATHLY

Mind is the most

intriguing, mysterious

yet the most disastrous and

deathly of man's possessions.

INFINITE POSSIBILITIES

Mind is an astonishing instrument,

no machinery is as complex,

yet so subtle;

with such infinite possibilities

POWER OF THE MIND

120

The way we use this instrument

or machinery called mind is completely up to us.

We can destroy it or utilize it positively

to its maximum potential.

Such is the power of the mind!

UNANSWERED QUESTIONS

No one who has walked this earth

has found a reasonable, logical

or even a remote answer

explaining intricacies of the creation

or unravelling layers of mysteries.

We ask why this, that, and the other,

but questions remain unanswered.

PANGS OF SEPARATION

Separation is an experience

that is joyful yet painful,

unbearable yet bearable;

makes the being alive, yet kills it,

the mystic pangs of separation.

PASSIONATE PAIN

123

No form of expression can describe

the passionate pain of separation like

repeated stabs piercing the wounds.

SERVE WITH HUMILITY

If we want to live in love,

we need to love others,

if we want to serve humanity

we need to serve with humility.

HARSH WORDS

125

Harsh words once uttered,

cannot be reversed,

they will scar and damage.

Words impact the person,

whether we repent

or ask for forgiveness.

POWERFUL TOOLS

126

Negative words are powerful tools

worse than body blows,

causing deep wounds.

CAUTION

127

Choose words carefully, cautiously!

Caution towards cutting words

Cut out the caustic words

PLAGUED

Innumerable memories plague me

Congesting the mind constantly

Some happy, some sad, others mad

Raking thoughts, I'd rather forget

Some vividly, crystal clear

Others foggy, yet sting with pain

Filling the mind with confusion

What to remember and what to forget